About the Author

Rosalind Edwards lives in the beautiful Eastern Cape of South Africa. She is the mother of six children and the wife of Zac. She has nine grandchildren to date, compliments of their three girls. Rosalind has been involved in the Mount Zion Sunday School for about 26 years. Her longing for children to learn to love biblical things motivated her to write these books.

Currently, Ros and Zac spend much of their free time metal-detecting on the beaches of the Indian Ocean, looking for pirates' treasure but finding mainly lead fishing weights, bottle caps, and pull tabs.

ROSALIND EDWARDS
ILLUSTRATED BY LUKE EDWARDS

THE RETOLD STORY OF
DAVID AND GOLIATH

AUSTIN MACAULEY PUBLISHERS®

LONDON • CAMBRIDGE • NEW YORK • SHARJAH

Ordering Information
Quantity sales: Special discounts are available on quantity purchases by corporations, associations, and others. For details, contact the publisher at the address below.

Publisher's Cataloging-in-Publication data
Edwards, Rosalind
The Retold Story of David and Goliath

ISBN 9798891555617 (Paperback)
ISBN 9798891555624 (ePub e-book)

Library of Congress Control Number: 2024915408

www.austinmacauley.com/us

First Published 2024
Austin Macauley Publishers LLC
40 Wall Street, 33rd Floor, Suite 3302
New York, NY 10005
USA

mail-usa@austinmacauley.com
+1 (646) 5125767

Dedications

As always, this book is dedicated to my family; each one of you is so very, very precious to me. And to my 'Sunday school' grandchildren, who inspire me to seek deeper as we discuss the wonderful things of God together.
To God be the glory.

Acknowledgements

I would like to acknowledge those who have encouraged me in the writing of my books: the matriarch of the Mount Zion Chapel, Sonia, and thank you for allowing me the privilege of being involved in the children's Sunday school; my biggest cheerleader and supporter, Lynne; and my family, who have always encouraged me and my passion so much.

Special acknowledgment to Luke, my son, who caught my vision so perfectly, and then, after discussions on my ideas for each illustration, managed to produce these beautiful drawings in a way I could never have imagined.

To those at Austin Macauley Publishers: Ms. Guevara for encouraging me to publish through AM Publishers and answering my many queries; Hazel Gilbert, who patiently coordinated the production; and to all the production team for their hard work and input. Your initial review of 'David' was really encouraging; thank you for believing we could do this!

David was a fine young man,
As fine as fine could be.
His day job that of shepherd boy,
So happy and so free.

To luscious fields of pastures green
Did David lead his sheep
To graze and lie down in the grass
Content to rest and sleep.

But danger always could lurk near –
A lion or a bear –
Who'd watch and wait to pounce upon
The lambs as they grazed there.

They stood no chance with David
He'd knock the mean beasts out.
He'd grab the lambkin from its jaw
Then raise a victory shout!

He gently led his rams and ewes
To safer stiller streams,
His watchful eye upon them as
They dreamed their sheepish dreams.

Then once a while would Dave's pa call,
"Come, to the front you go.
Deliver to your brothers 'cos
Provisions, they grow low."

Lunch pack in hand did David go
Food parcels to deliver
And most surprised was he to see
Men shaking, all a' quiver!

"What's up?" enquired our brave
young man,
"What's going on today?"
"A secret weapon have our foes!"
The frightened soldiers say.

"We are so scared!" the soldiers cried,
"Our hearts are melting fast
For the weapon of the Philistines is
A GIANT – huge and vast!"

"Goliath is this Philistine
Goliath, his name, we hear
He's nine feet tall and broad as well
Oh dear, oh dear, OH DEAR!!!"

"A giant?" fearless David asks,
"Surely not so bad,
'Cos we have our God on our side
Do not be bleak – be glad!"

"The God of Israel fights for us
This army is His own –
He'll fight this battle for our land.
Come stand! And stop your groans!"

"Who is this RIDICULOUS Philistine?
Has he not surely heard
He can't defy the armies
Of our true and living God."

Of all the soldiers in the land
The only voice that rose
Was that of David, shepherd boy,
Not scared of giant foes.

Good King Saul heard of this voice
That spoke above the rest.
"Bring him to me," he told his court,
"Can one man face this test?"

And David, fearless as before
Proclaimed his faith so fine,
A faith in God, his God, his King,
"HE'LL fight and win this time."

Then King Saul said, "Yes you're my man
Even though you're but a lad.
Take my armour, put it one
And FIGHT the giant bad."

The armour far too big it was
To fit on David's bod.
"I don't need this," he simply said,
"ALL THAT I NEED IS GOD!"

And armed with just five small round stones
And sling to throw them straight,
Off set our hero fearless boy
To fight the battle great.

"Who comes at me?" the giant roared,
"What cheek do they display!
A scrawny pipsqueak of a boy
Should fight me on this day!"

Then David braved this giant man
And spoke the truth, it seems.
"You think that sword and spear can save!
A javelin too! Oh please!!!"

"I come in the mighty name
Of God, the Lord of hosts.
The God of all of Israel
The God in whom I boast."

"You've dared defy our holy God
You scorn His servant boy.
This day will God defeat you
And your army we'll destroy!"

"This battle is not ours to fight
To win or lose this land.
THE BATTLE IS THE LORD'S you see
HE'LL deliver you to our hand."

G shook with rage as David stood
And trusty sling he swung.
Goliath tottered, lost his foot
And FELL; CRASH, BOOM and BANG!!!

Still no fear young David felt
To giant's still form he ran
And quick as lightning drew G's sword
And slew that giant man.

The army cheered, the nation glad
The battle won that day.
The God of Israel won the war
Praise Him alone, we say.

The faith of David turned the tide
Defeat to victory won
Because he trusted God his King
Praise God, praise Him, AMEN!!!

So...

If perchance, one day you feel
Quite scared as people can,
Remember how one little lad
Slew a huge great giant man.

How can that be – you well may ask
A stripling puts to flight
The largest foe that ever was
on any battle site.

The secret, we now know my friends,
the truth is plain to see
That God did guide young David's sling –
It's no big mystery

That David trusted God his King
He trusted God his Lord.
He trusted not in armour strong
Nor in a spear or sword.

Our God was on his side, you see
GOD fought the fight that day!
He helped young David shoot the stone
and send it on its way.

To save a whole great nation,
God made our hero bold.
To think that stone just hit its mark
And knocked the giant out cold!

For if our God is with you
Then nothing can compare
To His great strength and power
And a love so true and rare.

So don't you fret, dear children
God's with you all the way.
HE'LL fight your battles for you
For EVER and a day.

THE END